# ArT RANDOM

KYOTO SHOIN

First published in Japan 1989 by KYOTO SHOIN INTERNATIONAL Co., Ltd.
Sanjo-agaru, Horikawa, Nakagyo-ku, Kyoto, Japan. TEL[075]841-9123

Editorial director : Kyoichi Tsuzuki
Art director : Ichiro Miyagawa
Editorial coordinators : Midori Nishizawa, Edit deAk
© Copyright 1989 : Ray Smith

All works are reproduced by courtesy of Sperone Westwater Gallery, New York



ISBN4-7636-8547-3 C0371 P1980E

Printed and bound in Kyoto by SHASHIN KAGAKU Co., Ltd.

Photo : D. James Dee

cover : La Flautista, 1988
oil paint on pine  17 1/4" x 2 1/2" x 1 1/2"   front view

frontispiece : Pintura para mi Madre, 1989
oil on wood,  60" x 48"

# Ray Smith
# Sculpture

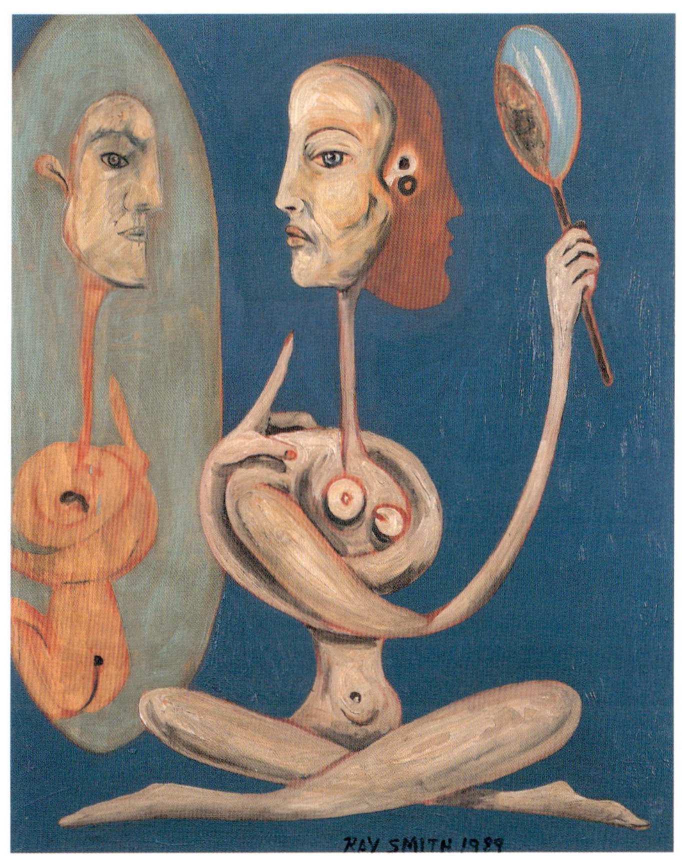


Edited by Midori Nishizawa

But beneath me, at the Equator, the earth pulses and beats like a

warrior's heart ;  till I know not, whether it be not myself.

And my soul sinks down to the depths, and soars to the skies ;

and comet-like reels on through such boundless expanses,

that methinks all the worlds are my kin,

and I invoke them to stay in their course.

Yet, like a mighty three-decker, towing argosies by scores,

I tremble, gasp, and strain in my flight,

and fain would cast off the cables that hamper.


And like a frigate, I am full with a thousand souls : and as on, on, on,

I scud before the wind, many mariners rush up from the orlop below,

like miners from caves ; running shouting across my decks ;

opposite braces are pulled ; and this way and that,

the great yards swing round on their axes ;

and boisterous speking trumpets are heard ;  and contending orders,

to save the good ship from the shoals.

Shoals, like nebulous vapours,

shoring the white reef of the Milky Way,

against which the wrecked worlds are dashed ;

strewing all the strand with their Himmaleh keels and ribs.


Ay : many, many souls are in me.


Herman Melville
*Mardi and a Voyage Thither* Vol II, Ch.XV  "Dreams"  pg.53

Viviem em nós inúmeros,
Se penso ou sinto, ignoro
Quem é que pensa ou sente.
Sou somente o lugar
Onde se sente ou pensa.


Tenho mais almas que uma.
Há mais eus do que eu mesmo.
Existo todavia
Indiferente a todos,
Faço-os calar: eu falo.


Os impulsos cruzados
Do que sinto ou não sinto
Disputam em quem sou.
Ignoro-os. Nada ditam
A quem me sei : eu 'screvo.


Ricardo  Reis
( Fernando Pessoa)

from *Odes de Ricardo Reis*, Fernando Pessoa

1.  Escultura #1, 1986   painted wood    51 3/4" x 24  1/4 " x 4 1/2"

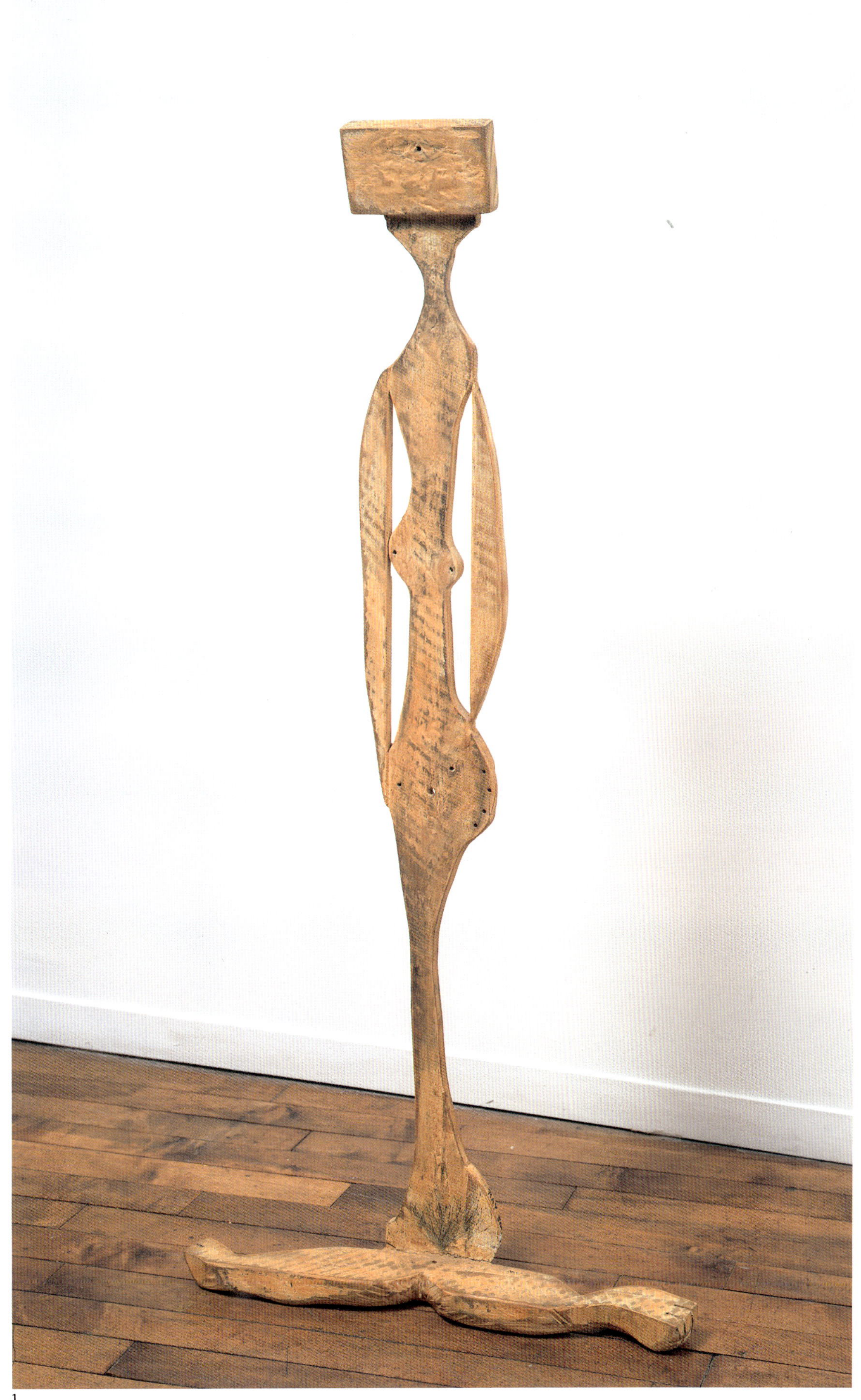

1

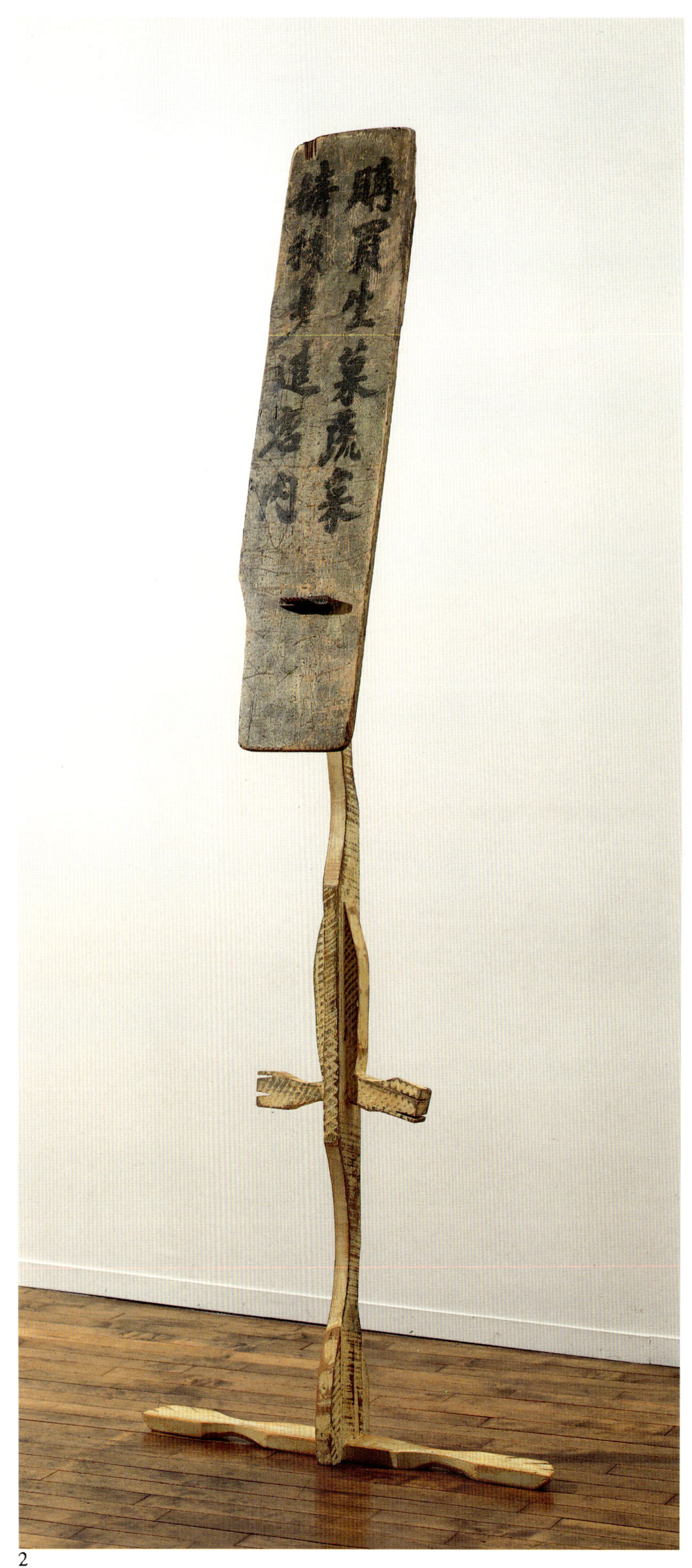


2

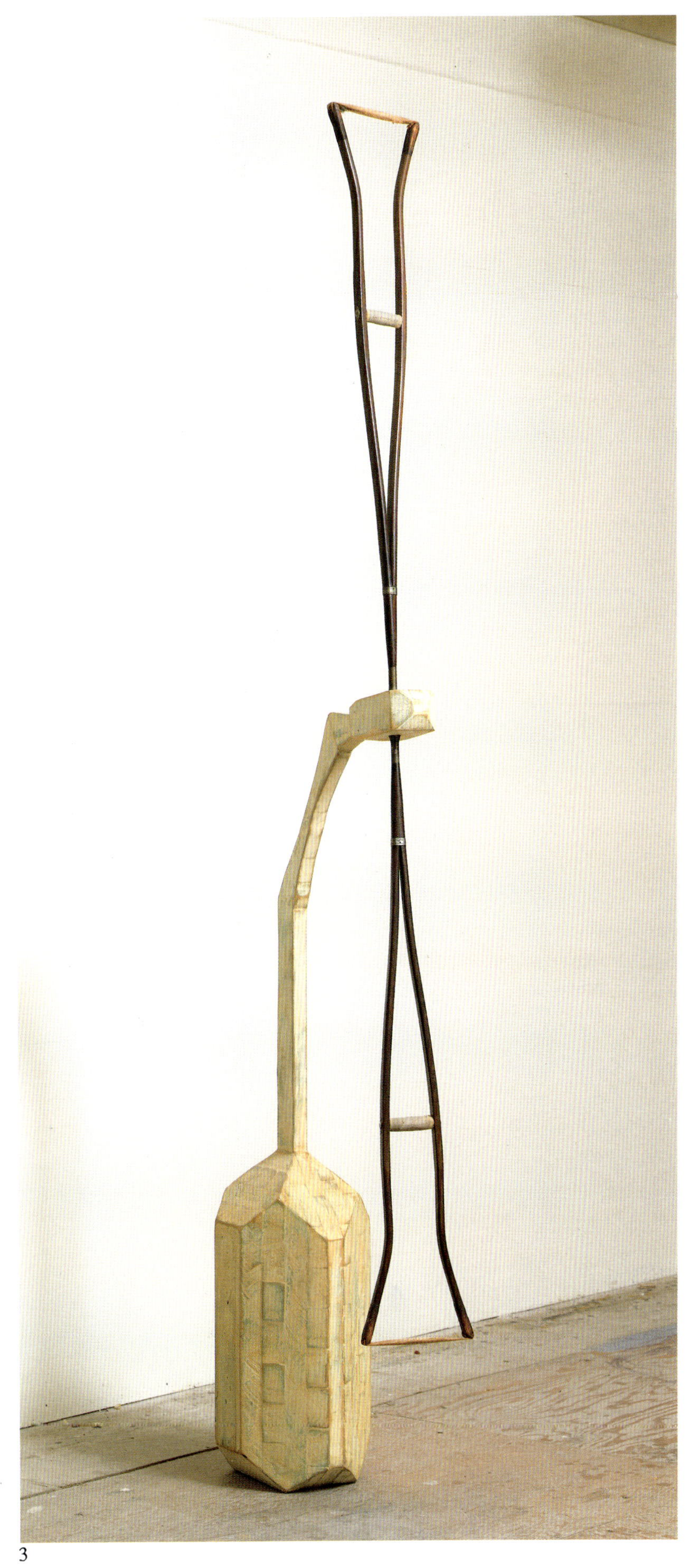

3

2. Elchino, 1987   wood and steel   113" x 41" x 7  1/2"

3. Monumento a los Invalidos de la Aeronautica, 1988   wood, cloth and steel  121 1/2" x 12 1/2" x 17"

4.La Enfermera, 1987   wood and steel   151"x 26"x 30"

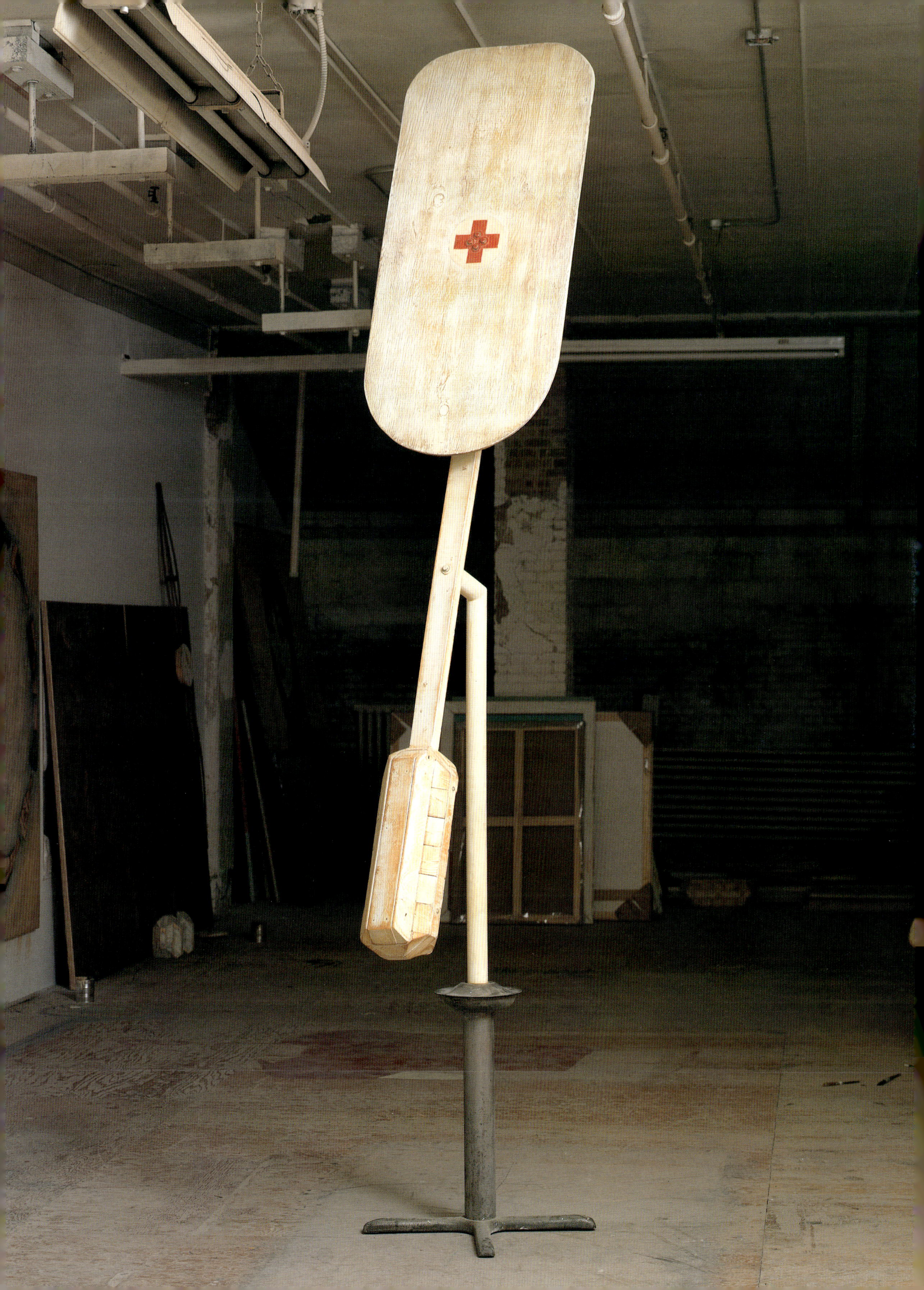

5.Parejade Palos, 1987  left: rubber, wood and ceramic  93"x 17"x 14"  right: wood  90 1/2"x 11 1/2"x 7 1/4"

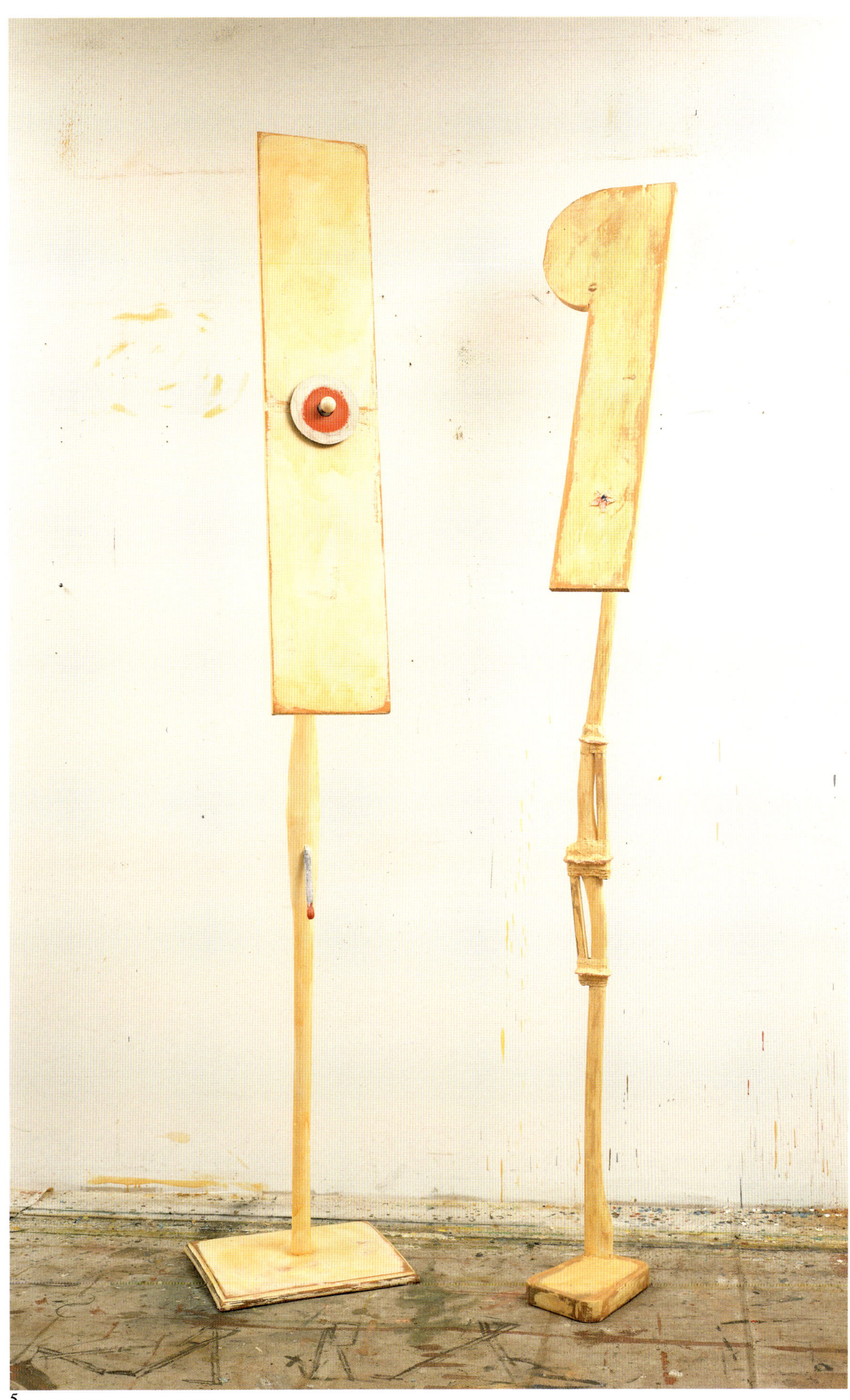

6. Figura Muletas, 1988    wood, steel and plaster   116"x 8"x 2"

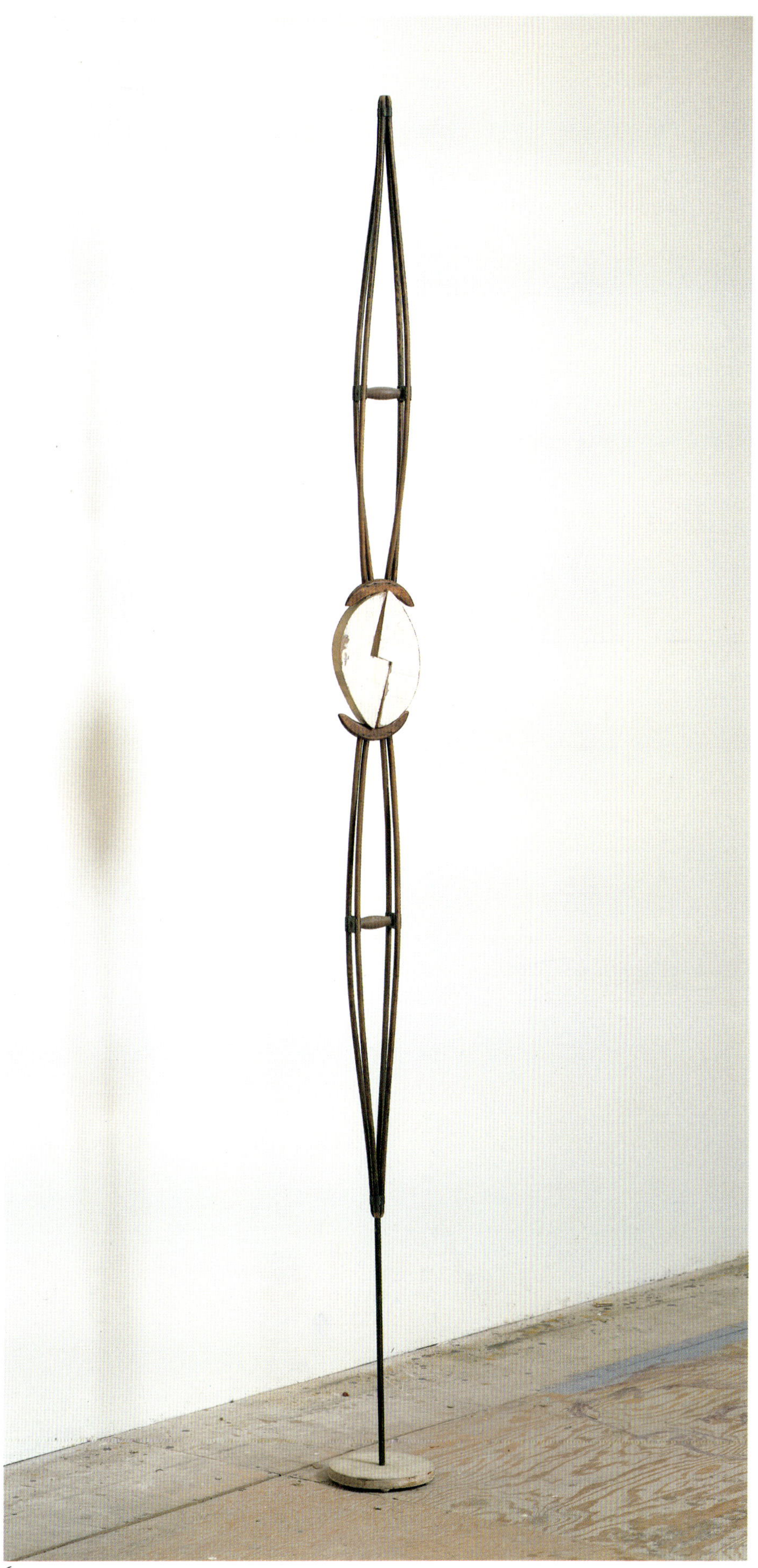

7. Figura Reclinada, 1987   wood and steel   75"x 36"x 88 1/2"

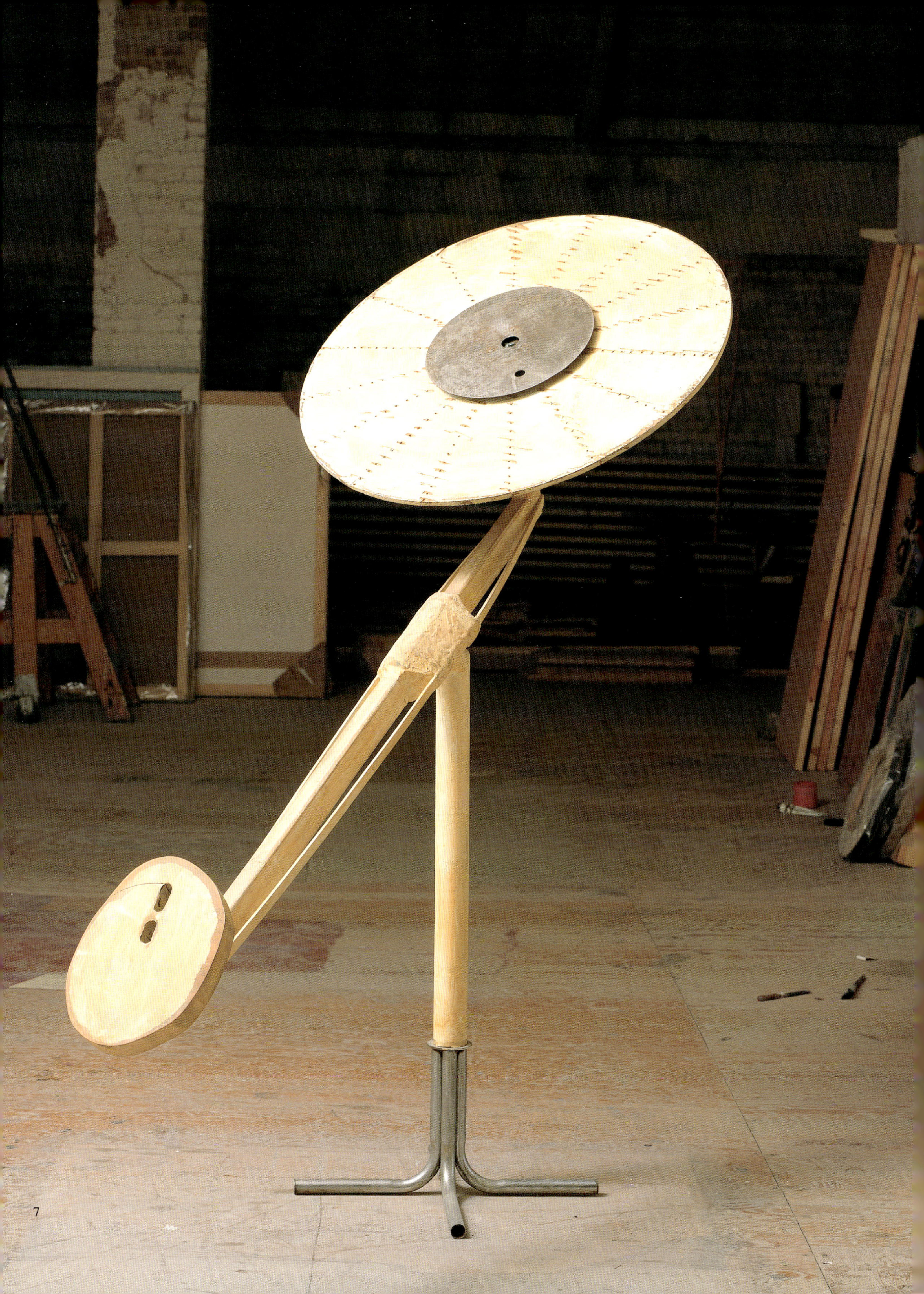

8. Poseidon, 1988   wood and steel   78"x 16"x 7"

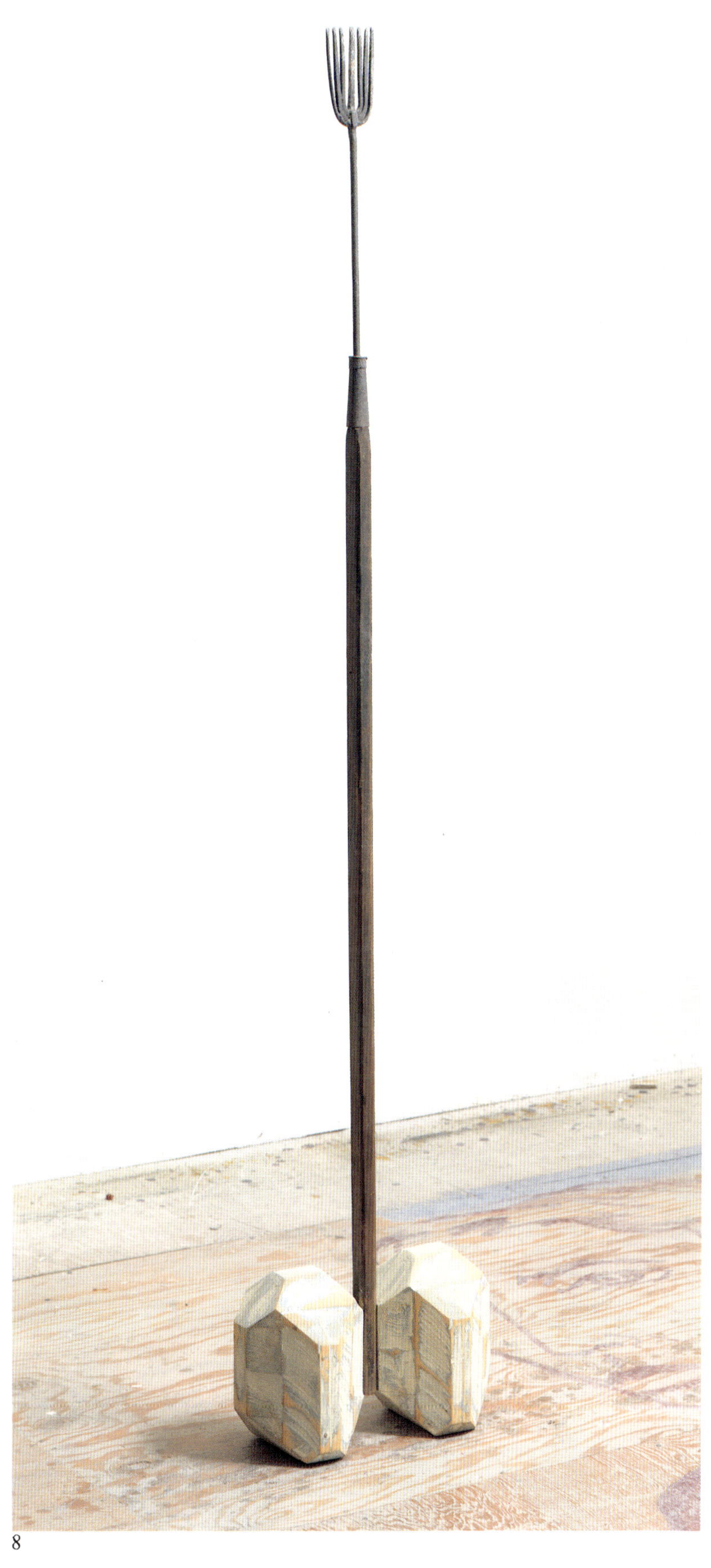

8

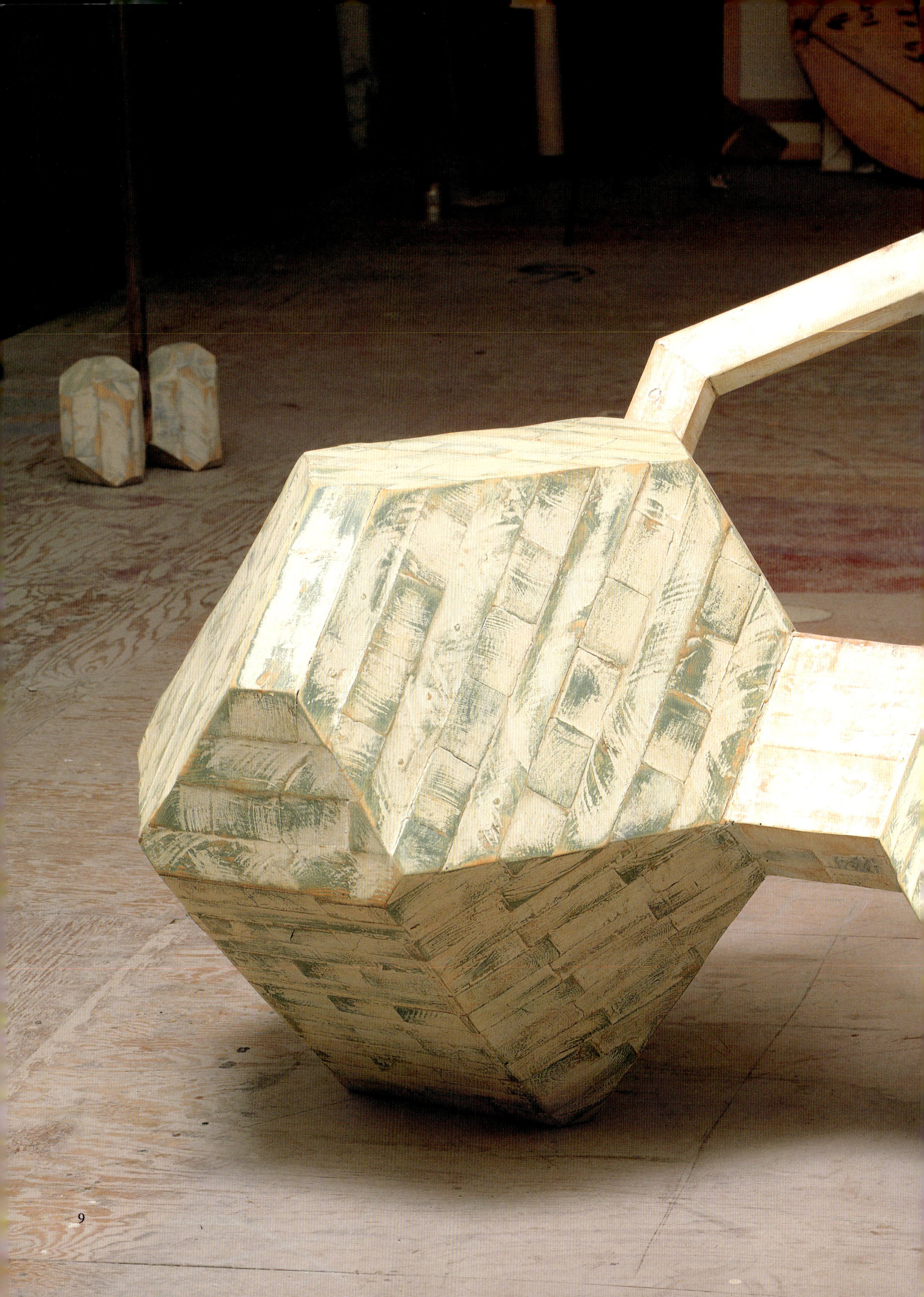

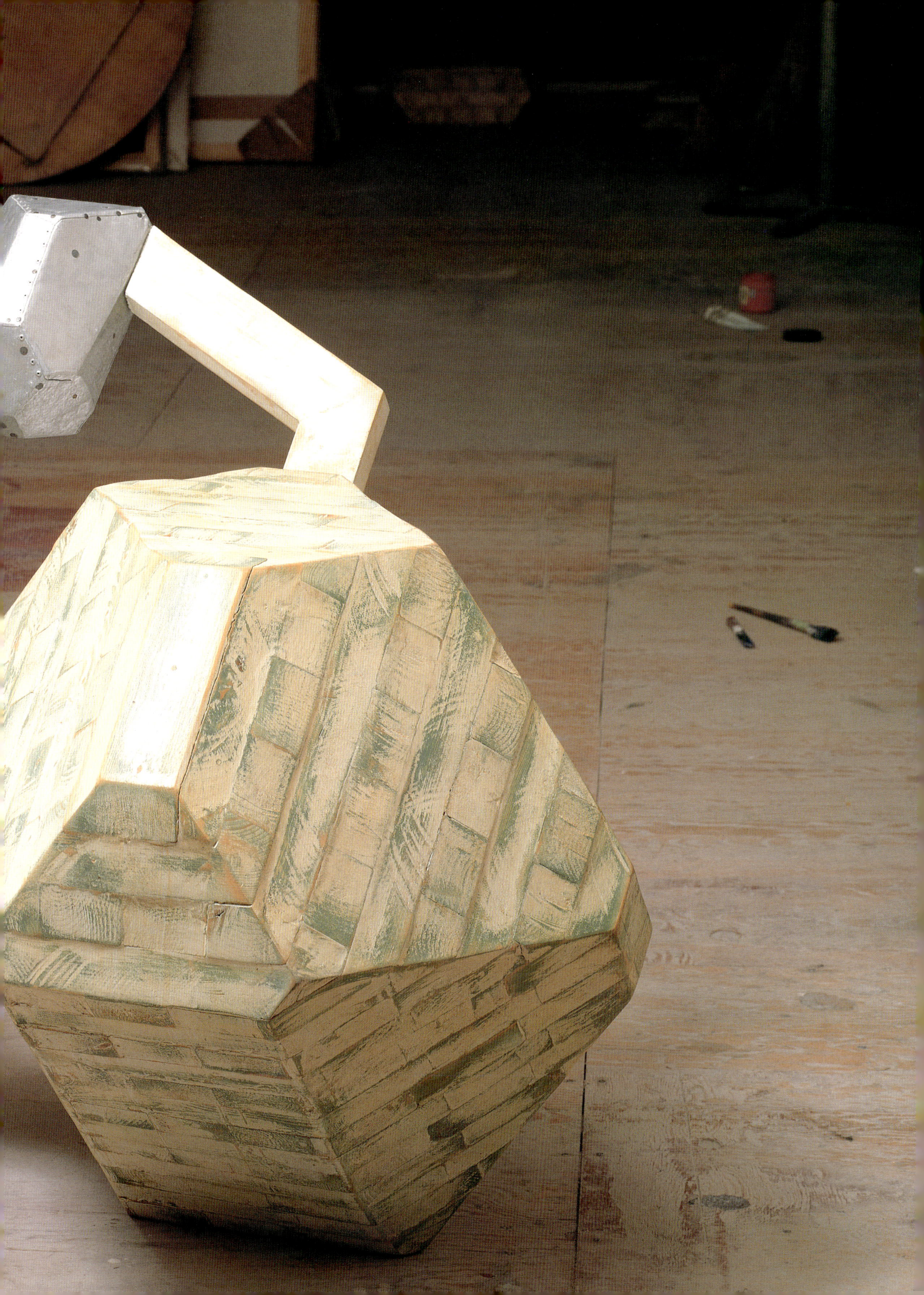

9.Chico Huevon, 1988   wood and aluminum   38"x 46"x 70"

10. La Portera, 1988    wood and steel    61"x 90"x 10 1/2"

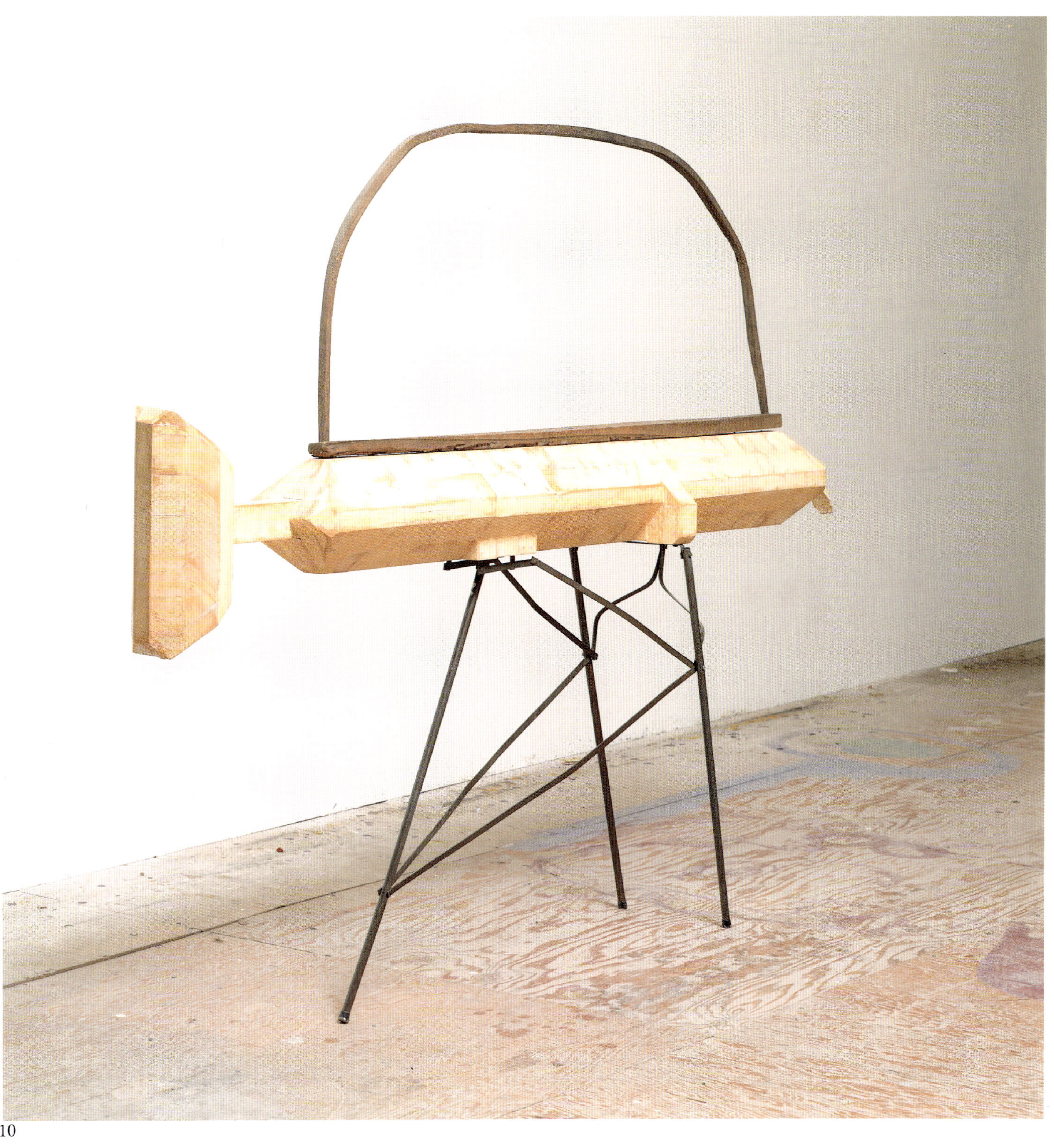

11. El Benemerito, 1988   wood and steel   108"x 24 1/2"x 24 1/2"

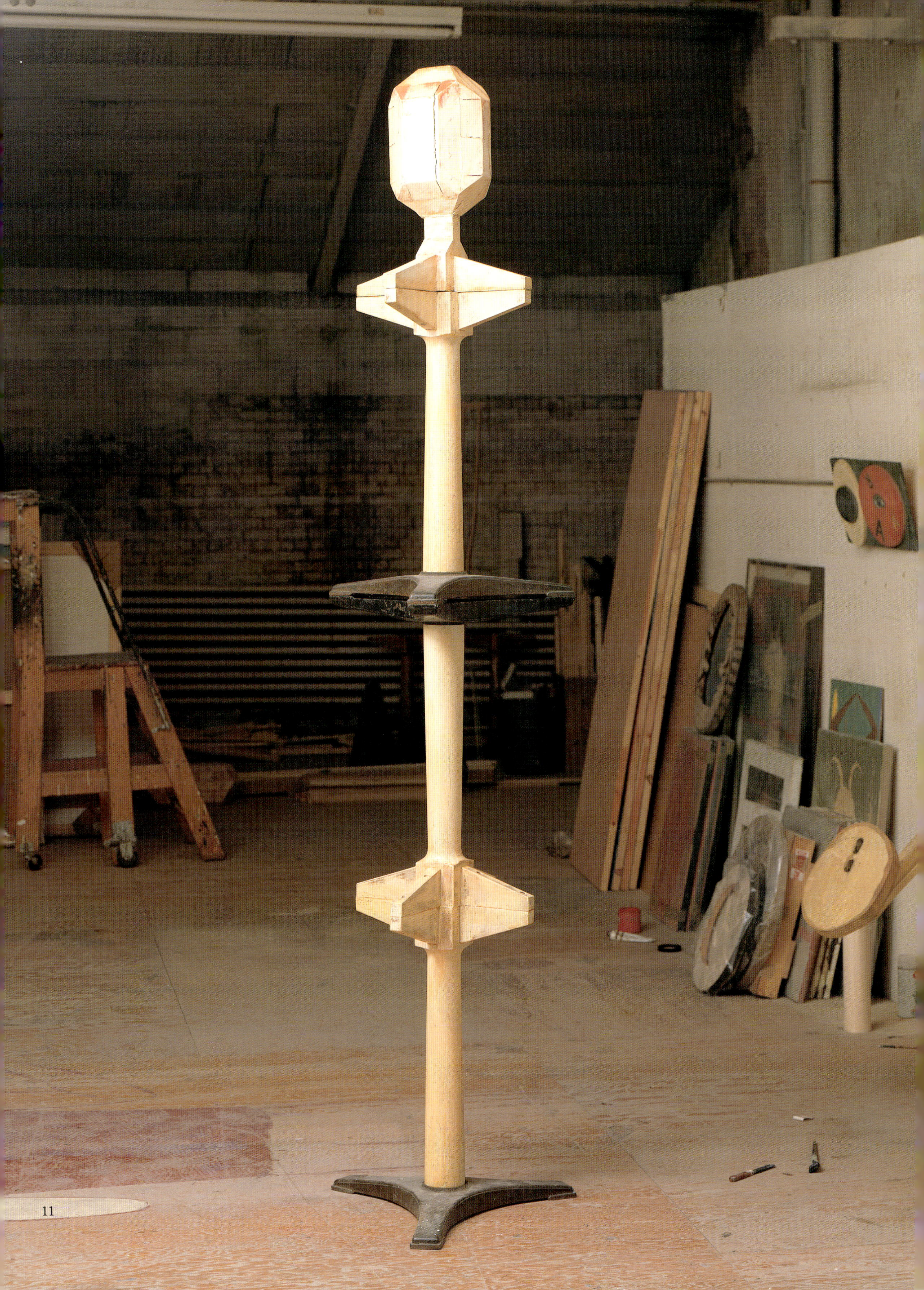

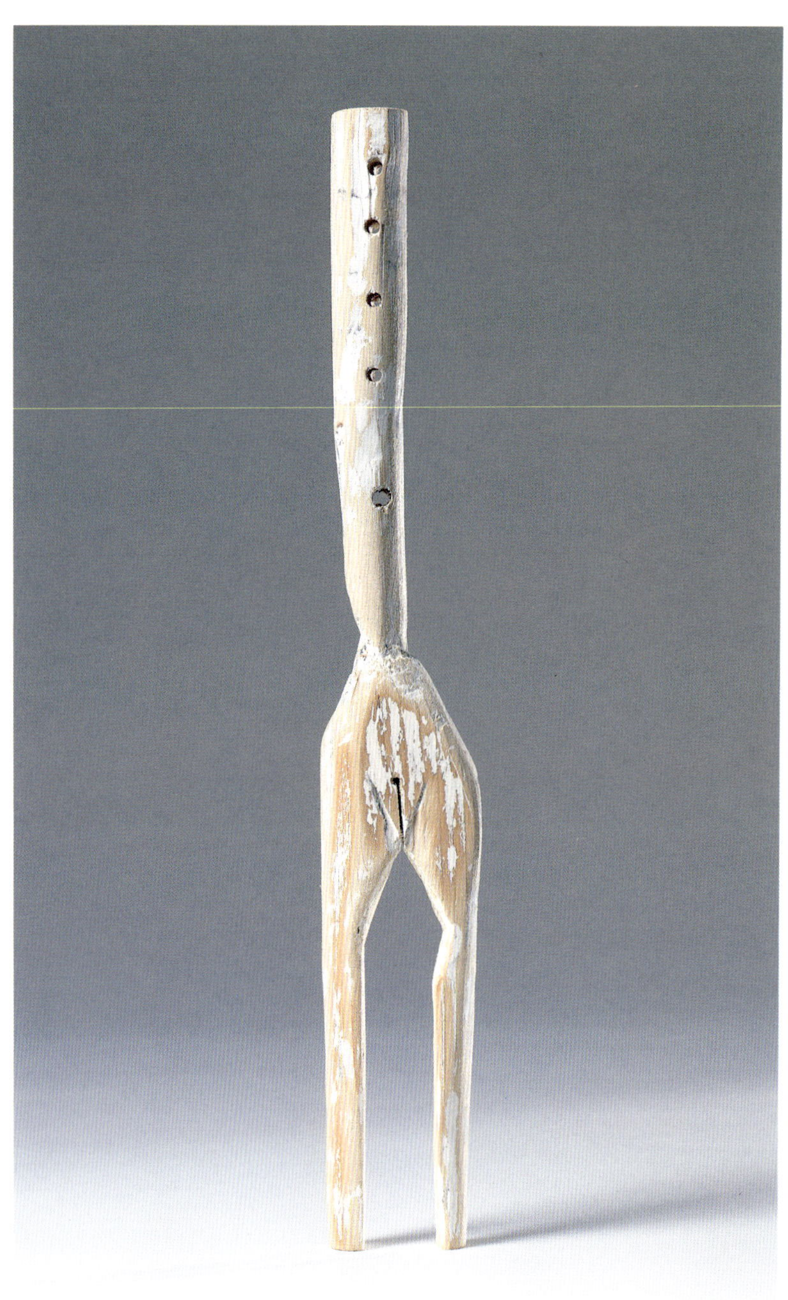

12

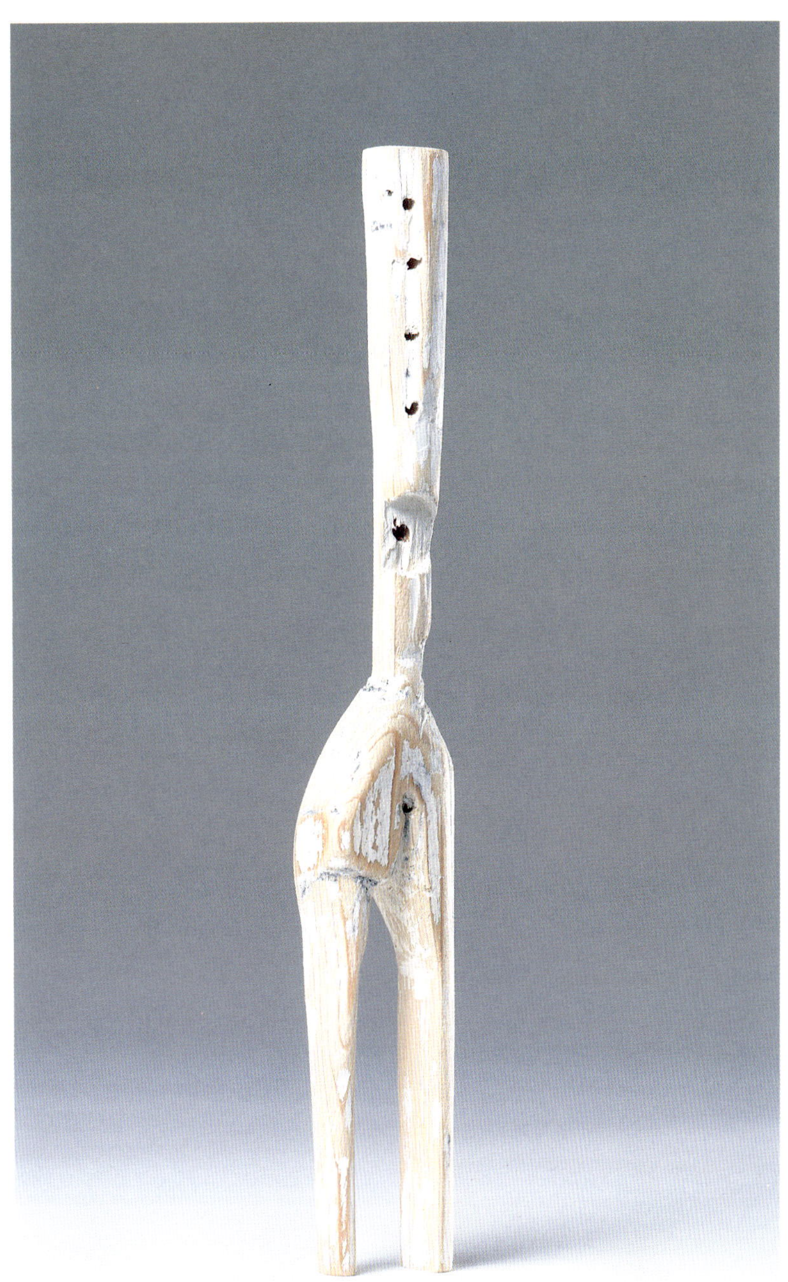

13

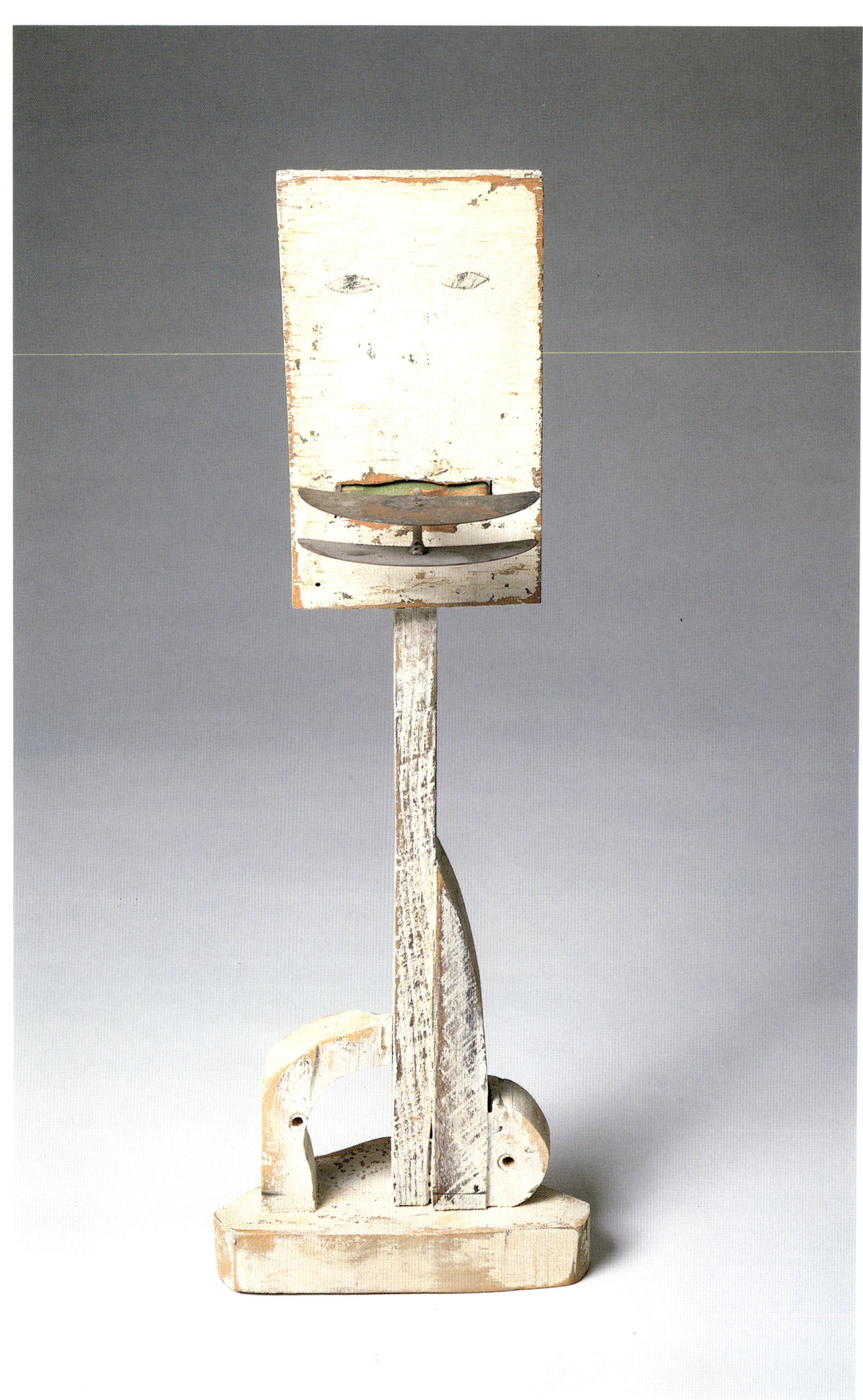

14

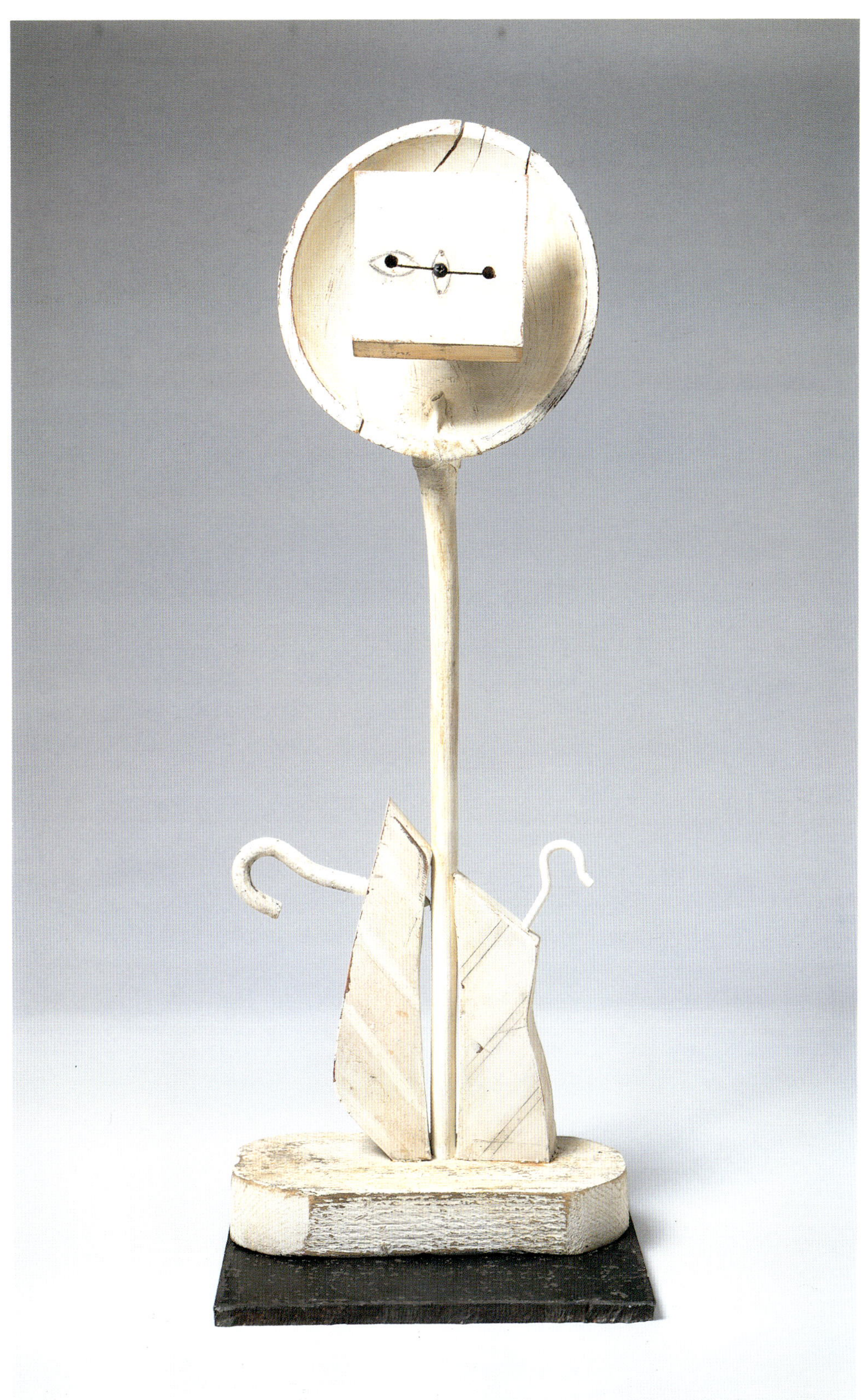

15

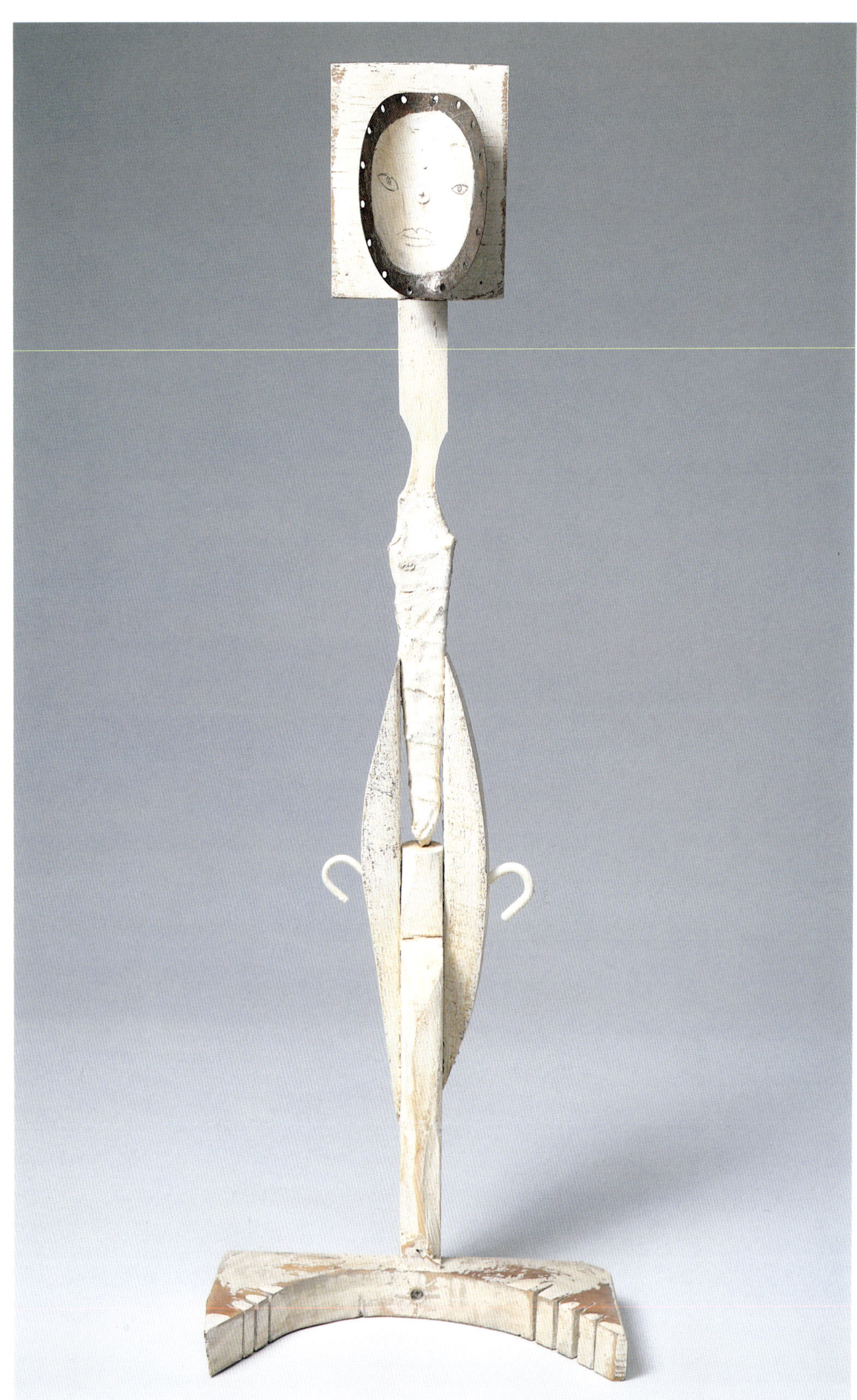

16

12. La Flautista, 1988   oil paint on pine   17 1/4"x 2  1/2"x 1 1/2"   front view

13. La Flautista, 1988   oil paint on pine   17  1/4"x 2  1/2"x 1 1/2"   back view

14. Figura Africana, 1989   oil paint on wood and steel   27 1/2" x 10" x 5"

15. Busto De Mujer, 1989   oil paint on wood and steel   36 1/2" x 14" x 6 1/2"

16. Mujer Sentada, 1989   oil paint on wood and steel   42 1/2" x 14 1/4" x 10"

17. Untitled, 1989   wood and steel   84" x 9 1/2" x 9 1/2"

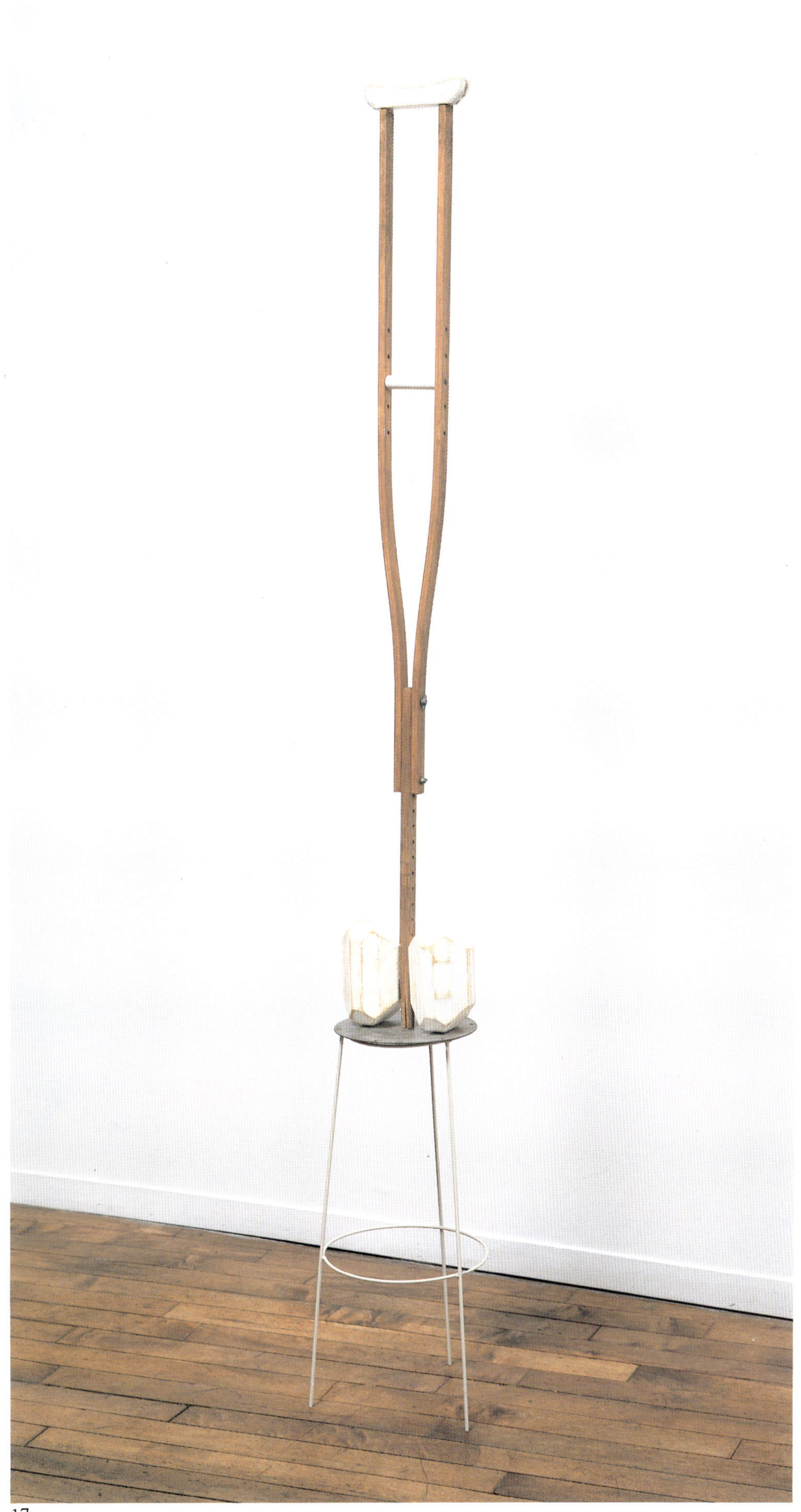

18. Patzcuaro, 1986   wood and steel   52" x 40" x 7 1/2"

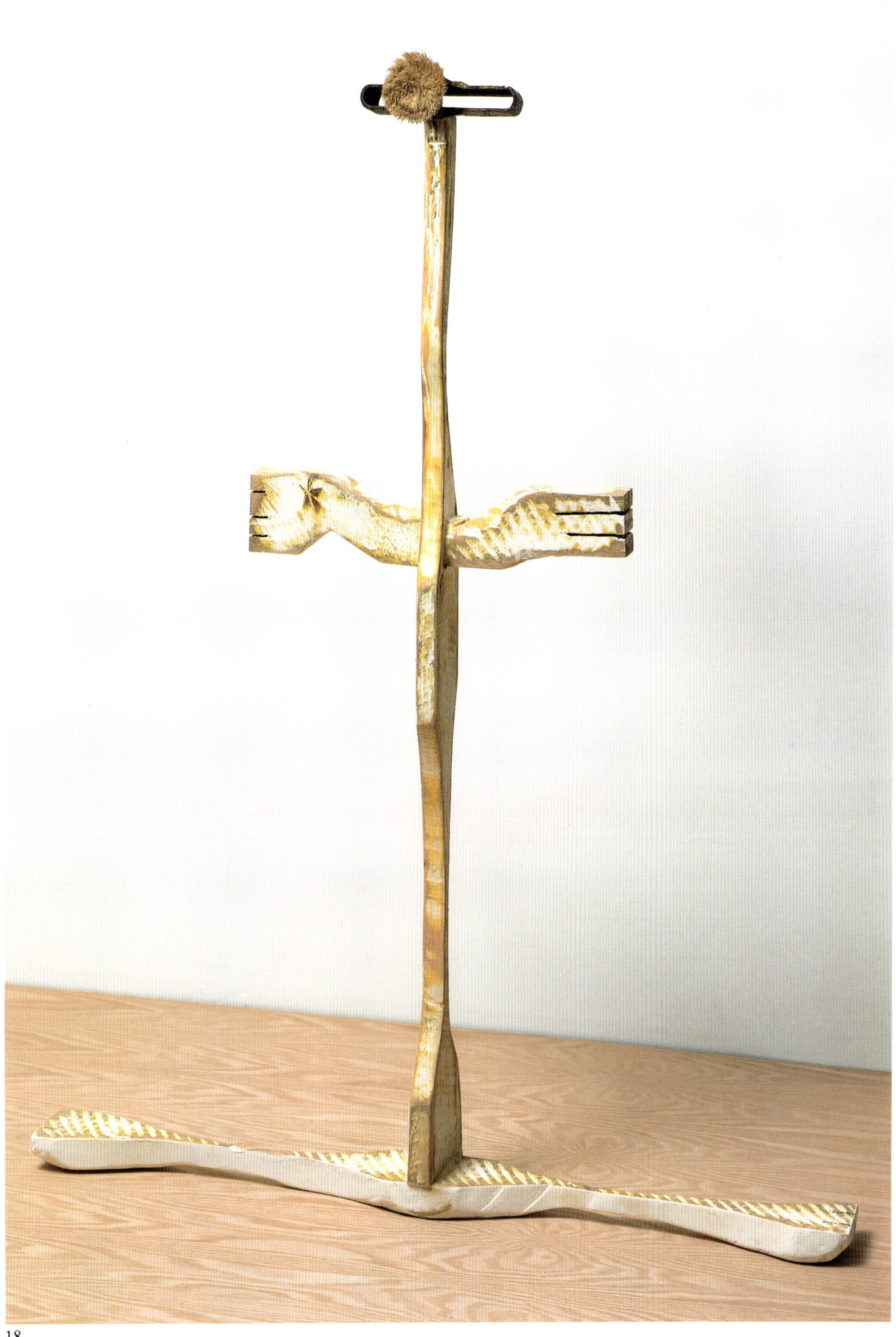

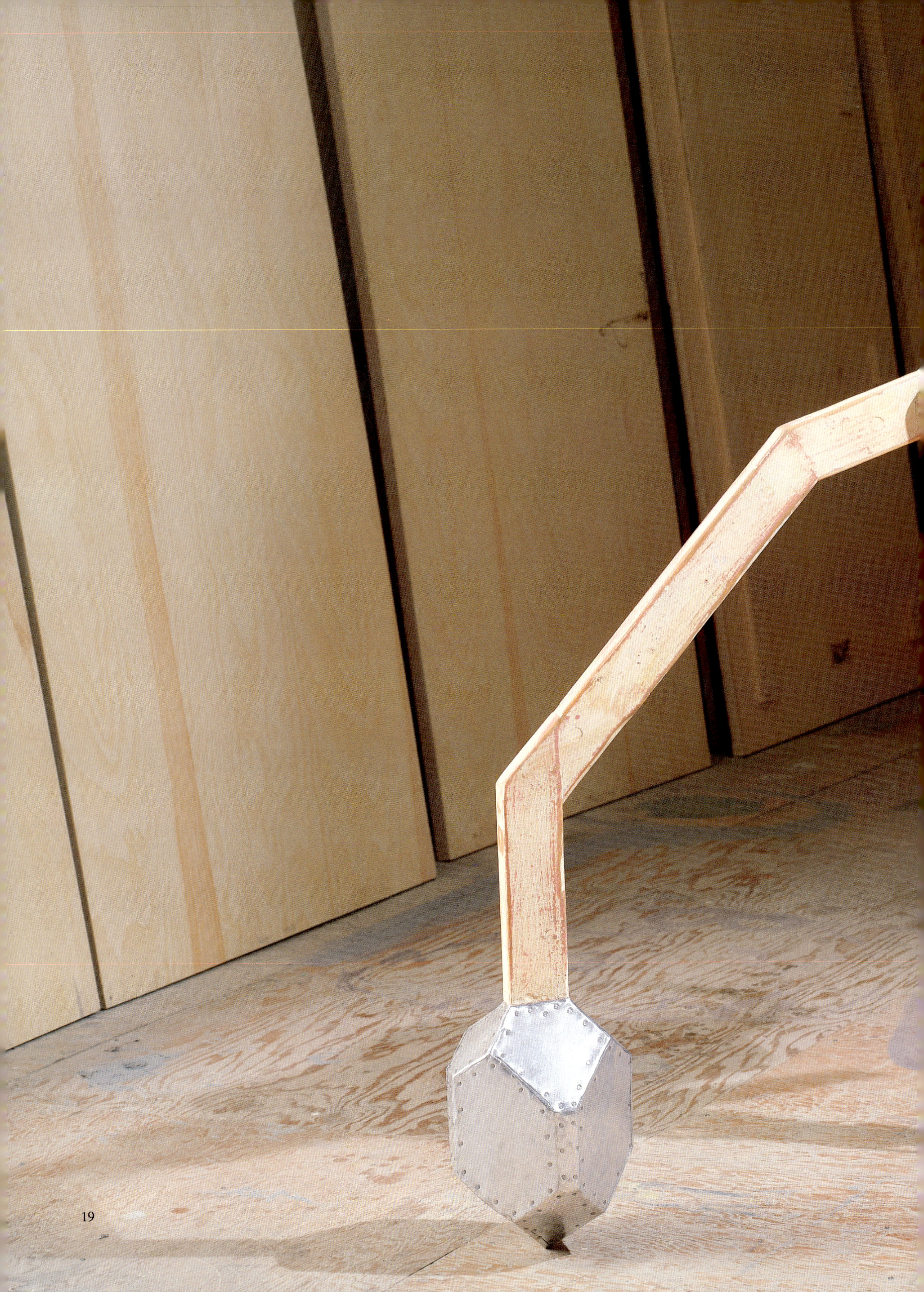

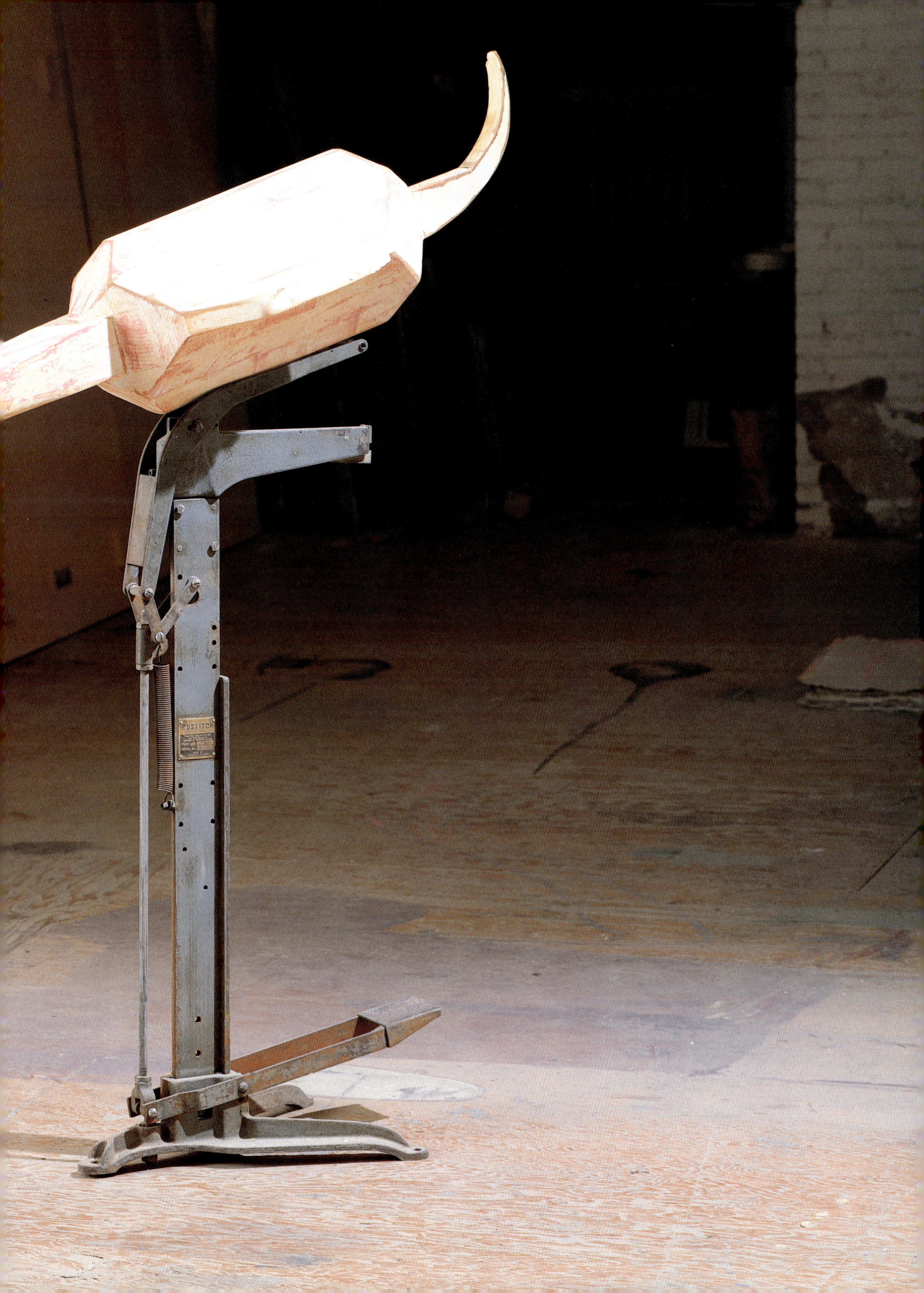

19. Pollo Pekin, 1989   oil paint on wood and steel   63" x 61" x 18"

20. La Lechera, 1989   wood, steel and glass   104" x 11 3/4" x 19"

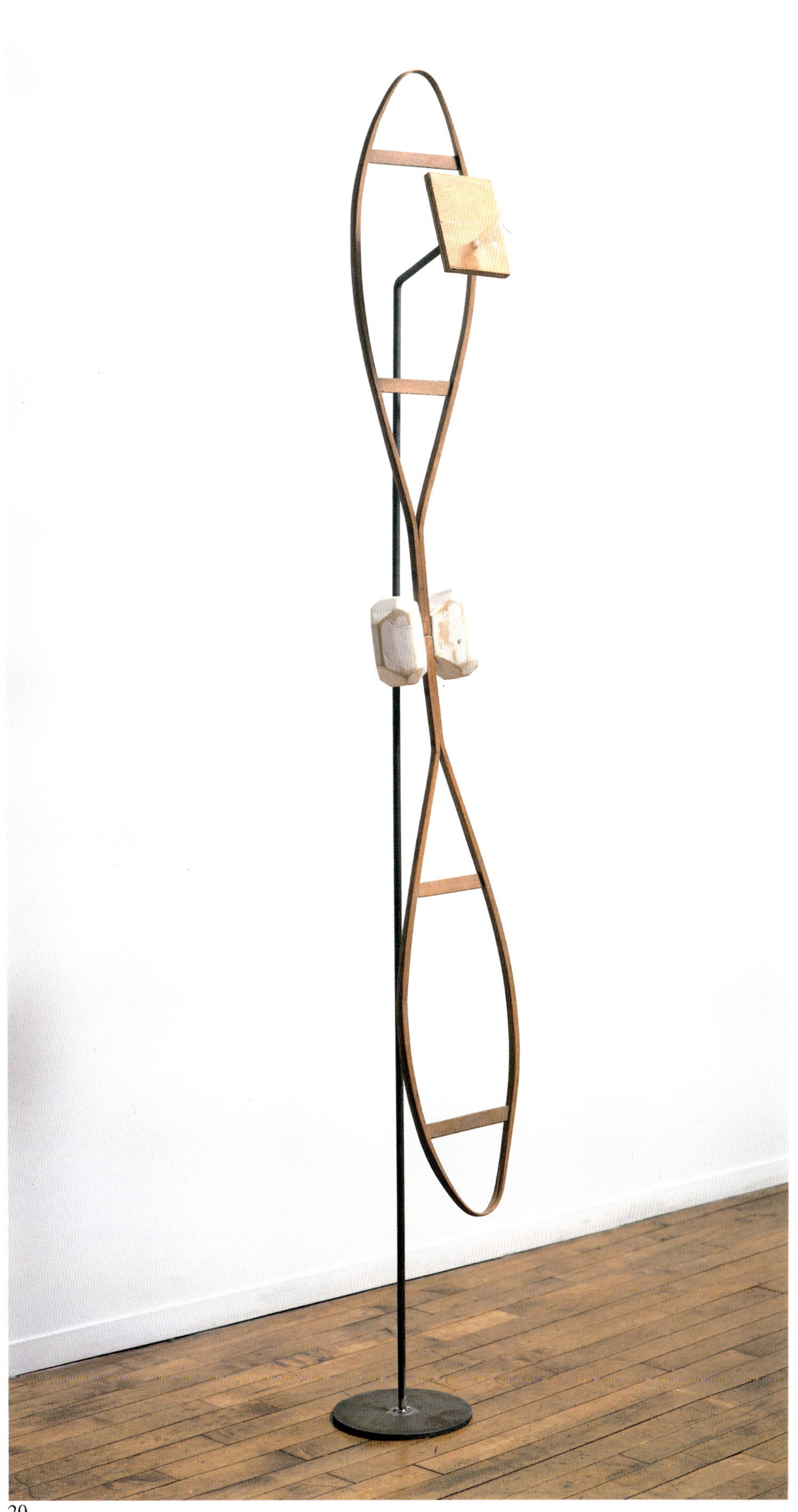

21. Mujer De Angola, 1989   wood and steel   120" x 22" x 20"

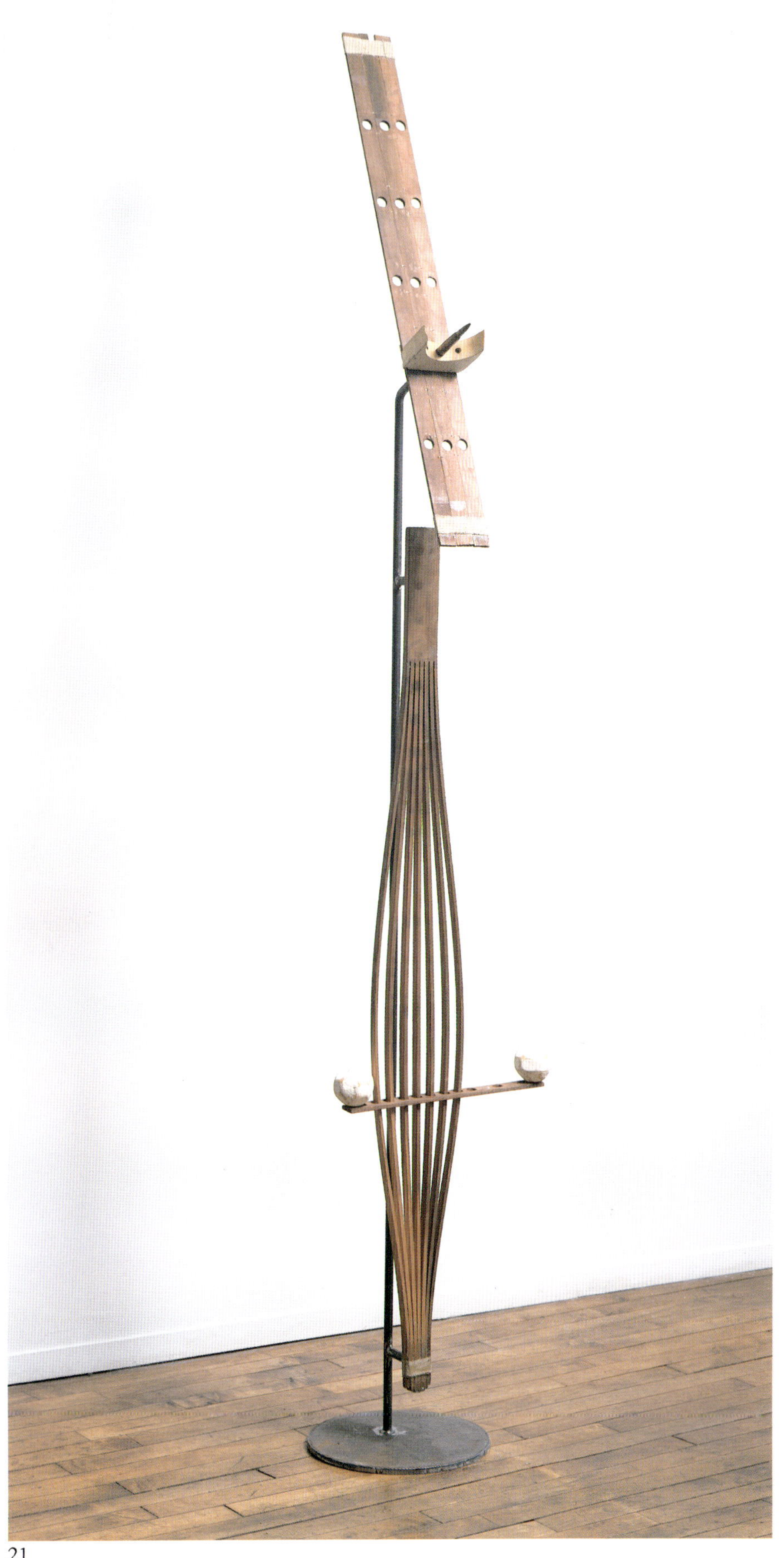

21

22. Mujer Encinta, 1989   wood and steel   104 1/2" x 17" x 17"

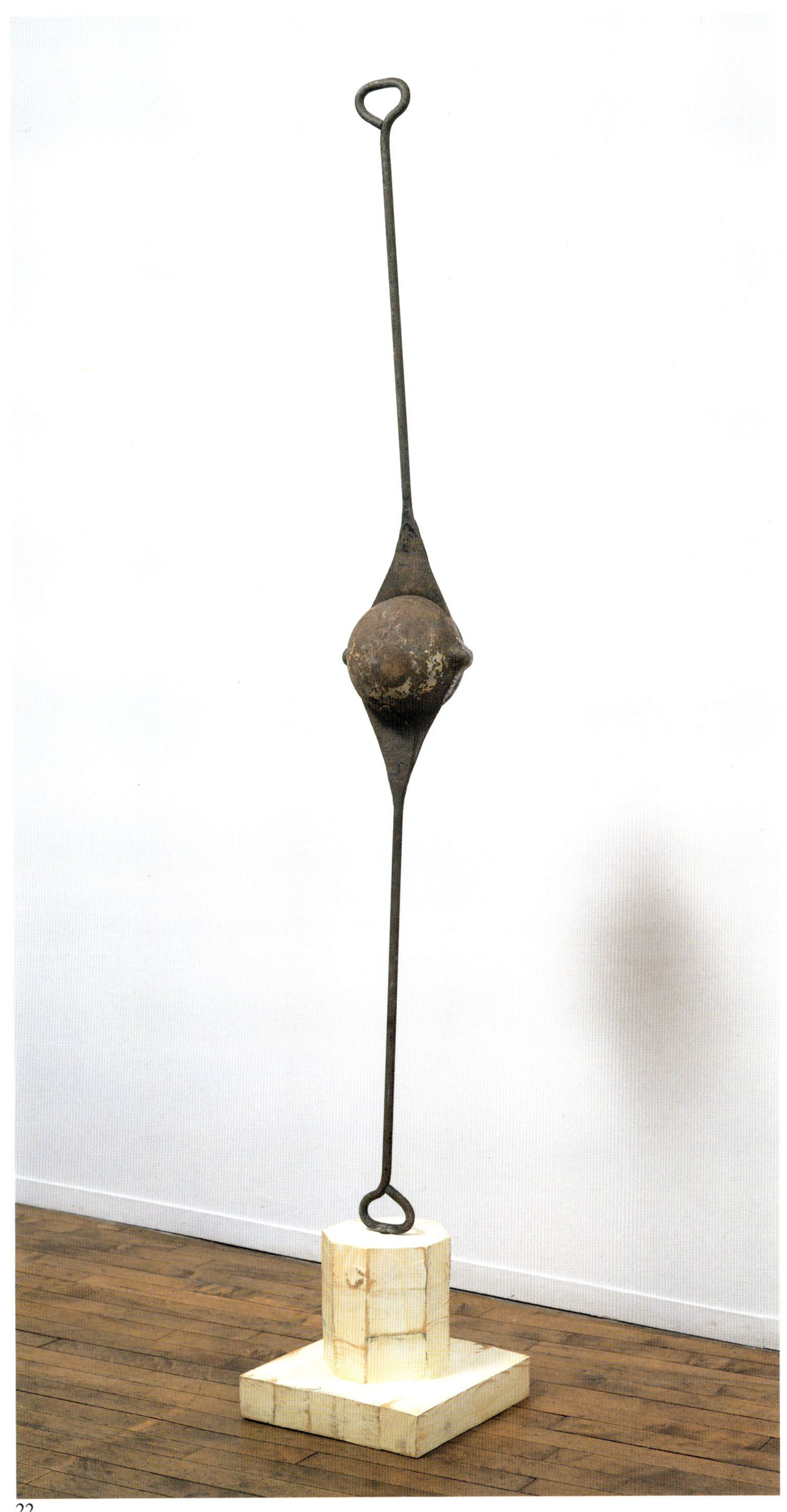

22

23. Trompo Africano, 1989   wood and steel   120" x 16 1/4" x 15 1/2"

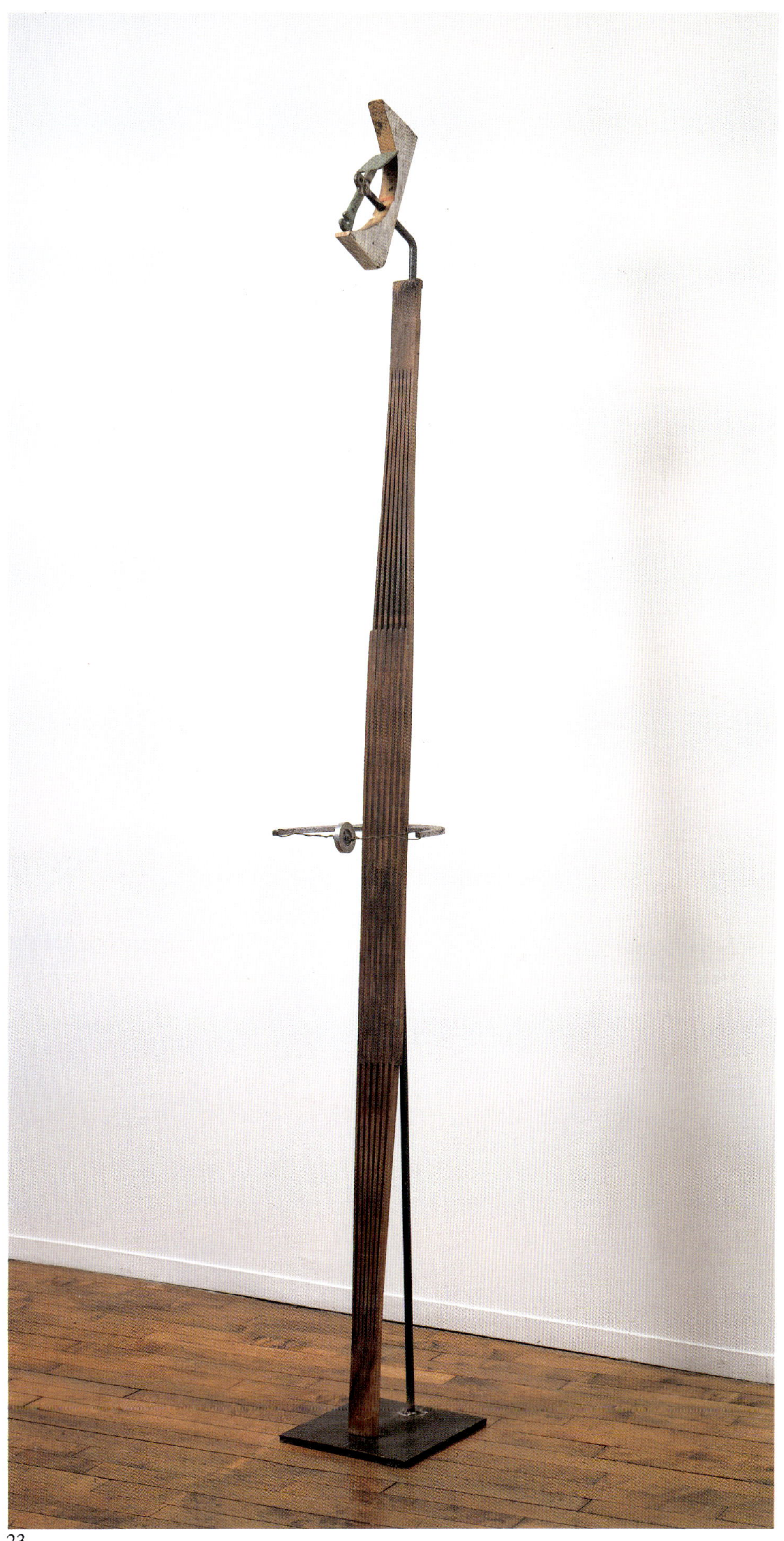

　だが、ぼくの下では、赤道直下、地球が激しく脈動するのが聞こえる。武士の心臓か！ついには地球がぼく自身ではないとは言えなくなる。するとぼくの魂は沈んで沈んで深海に落ち、また跳躍して中天に飛翔する。ぼくは流星となって、この広大無辺の無の空間を流転また流転し、ついには、全世界が己の家族だと思い、全世界が現在の路線を永久不変に保ってくれと神呼びする。それでもまだ、巨大な三層軍艦が数十隻の大商船隊を曳き船してゆく時がそうであるように、ぼくは震え、呻き、逃竄のヒズミに耐えかね、つまずきの絆となっているこの纜を切ろうともがく。

　そしてまた快足艦のように幾千の魂を抱いて溢れんばかりだ。まっしぐらに、ただまっしぐらに、風を切って進むぼくの内側では、大勢のマドロスが最下甲板から飛び出してくるのが炭坑から出てくる坑夫のようで、大声で叫びながらぼくの甲板を駆けめぐる。反対の舷をトリムするものだから、巨大な円材があちらこちらへ軸を中心に揺れては回る。けたたましいメガフォンの声も聞こえる。浅瀬から船を救えとのちぐはぐな命令だ。浅瀬は星雲の靄めき、《銀河》のま白き岩礁に接して連なり、破船した全世界はこれにあたって玉砕、砕けた残骸は岸べに散らばり、ヒマラヤの竜骨も肋材もこっぱ微塵だ。

　そうなんだ！ぼくの内なるところには、数かぎりない魂が宿されているのだ。

『マーディ』第119章より、坂下昇訳、国書刊行会、メルヴィル全集第4巻

我々の内なる　数知れない存在

考えたことや感じたことが、

私の中の誰によるものなのか

私は知らない

私は

感覚と思考の舞台


私は複数の「魂」を持つ

私以外の「私達」がいる

それでも私は存在する

私以外の私には一切関せず、

彼らの口を封じ、私を語る私がいる


さまざまな衝動が、思い出がぶつかり

交差し、私の内で矛盾しあう

それでいい、私は私だ

彼らとは違う私、この私が

今、書いているのだ

『リカルド・ライスの頌』フェルナンド・ペソア、訳：西澤みどり

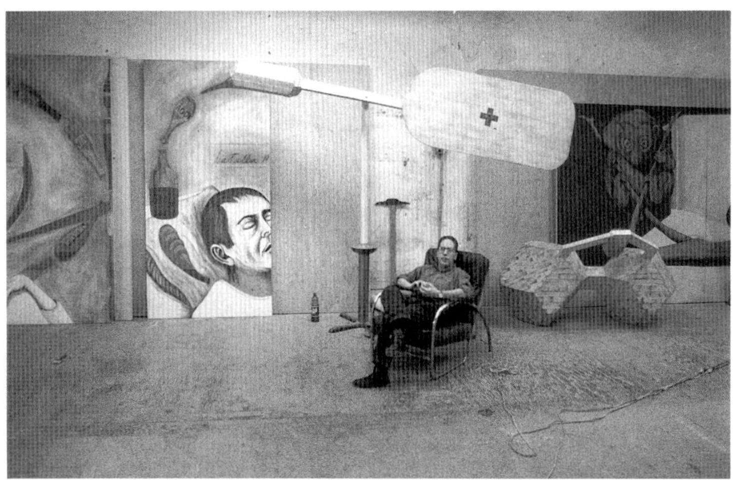

Ray Smith at his studio, 1989

**Ray Smith**
Painter. Born in Brownsville, Texas, in 1959.
Currently lives and works in Mexico City and New York.

**Fernando Pessoa**
Poet. Born in Lisbon, 1888. Pessoa wrote poems under three main 'personae':
Albert Caeiro, Ricardo Reis, and Alvaro de Campos. He died in 1935.